Y0-EJO-550

WITHDRAWN

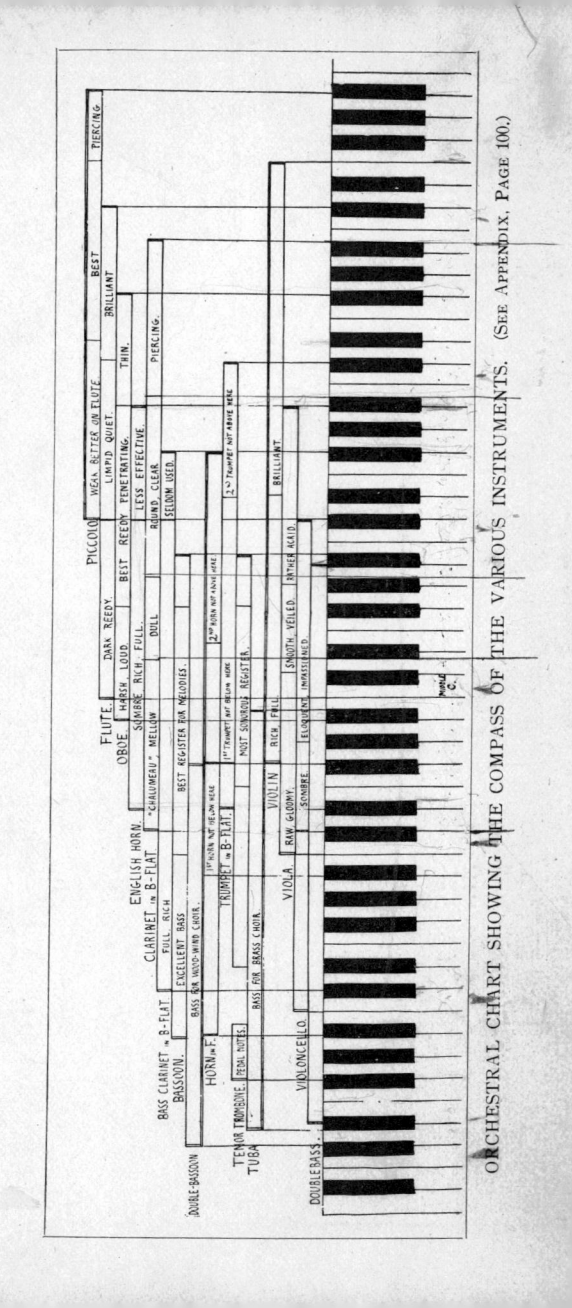

ORCHESTRAL CHART SHOWING THE COMPASS OF THE VARIOUS INSTRUMENTS. (SEE APPENDIX, PAGE 100.)

The Orchestral Instruments and What They Do

A Primer for Concert-Goers

BY

DANIEL GREGORY MASON

NEW YORK
THE BAKER & TAYLOR CO.
1909

Copyright, 1908, by The H. W. Gray Co.

Copyright, 1909, by The H. W. Gray Co.

FIRST PUBLISHED IN THE NEW MUSIC REVIEW

PREFATORY NOTE.

The object of this little book is to assist the concert-goer in recognizing the various orchestral instruments, both by sight and by hearing, and to stimulate his perception of the thousand and one beauties of orchestral coloring. As a help to the eye, the descriptions of the appearance of the instruments are supplemented by pictures; in order to help recognition by ear, the divers registers of instruments are discussed with some particularity; while it is hoped that the many figures showing excerpts from standard works will sharpen the reader's attentiveness to delicate shades of tonal effect.

These excerpts should serve only as an introduction to full scores of a few standard works, which can now be bought at moderate prices in miniature size, and which are of the greatest use in defining and regulating the act of listening, even for those who can read music only in the most tentative, stumbling way. Suggestions are given in Section XX as to the use of scores by those who can do no more than count time, recognize accents, and see whether the tune is "going up or down."

There are few persons fond enough of music to attend orchestral concerts who would not find in a few months their powers of musical enjoyment doubled or trebled by the study of scores. Especially in large cities where symphonic works may often be heard more than once in one season, the study of scores between performances, combined with a sharp scrutiny of the orchestra during the concerts, is capable of increasing appreciation of the music to a remarkable degree.

The illustrations of the orchestral instruments were obtained through the kind coöperation of Mr. Walter Damrosch, to whom the author desires to express his thanks. Grateful acknowledgement is also made of the trouble taken by the following gentlemen in sitting for the photographs: Mr. David Mannes and Mr. Rudolf Rissland, violin; Mr. Romain Verney, viola; Mr. Paul Kefer, violoncello; Mr. L. E. Manoly, double-bass; Mr. B. Fanelli, harp; Mr. G. Barrère, flute; Mr. Albert de Busscher, oboe; Mr. Irving Cohn, English horn; Mr. H. L. Leroy, clarinet; Mr. Louis Haenisch, bass clarinet; Mr. August Mesnard, bassoon; Mr. Richard Kohl, contrabass clarinet; Mr. Herman Hand, French horn; Mr. Max Bleyer, trumpet; Mr. Sam Tilkin, trombone; Mr. Fred. Geib, tuba; Mr J. F. Sietz, kettledrums, and Messrs. George Wagner, Emil Hönnig and Fred. Rothery for the instruments of percussion.

CONTENTS

	PAGE
CHAPTER I. The Orchestra as a Whole	7
SECTION I. The Nature of Sound	7
SECTION II. Constitution of the Orchestra	12
SECTION III. A Bird's-eye View of the Orchestra	16
CHAPTER II. The Stringed Instruments	20
SECTION IV. The Stringed Instruments	20
SECTION V. The Violin	21
SECTION VI. The Viola	29
SECTION VII. The Violoncello	31
SECTION VIII. The Double-bass	35
CHAPTER III. The Wood-wind Instruments	39
SECTION IX. The Wood-wind Instruments	39
SECTION X. The Flute	40
SECTION XI. The Oboe	45
SECTION XII. The Clarinet	52
SECTION XIII. The Bassoon	60
CHAPTER IV. The Brass Instruments	64
SECTION XIV. The Brass Instruments	64
SECTION XV. The Horn	64
SECTION XVI. The Trumpet	74
SECTION XVII. The Trombones and Tuba	77
CHAPTER V. The Percussion Instruments	83
SECTION XVIII. The Percussion Instruments	83
CHAPTER VI. Orchestral Combinations	86
SECTION XIX. Orchestral Combinations	86
CHAPTER VII. Scores and Score-reading	95
SECTION XX. Scores and Score-reading	95
APPENDIX. The Orchestral Chart	100

THE ORCHESTRAL INSTRUMENTS
AND
WHAT THEY DO

CHAPTER I.

I.—THE NATURE OF SOUND.

From the point of view of the physical scientists, the orchestra is nothing but a large and very complicated machine for setting the air in motion. All sound, they tell us, is produced only by pulsations or puffs of air, and can move through space only because air is elastic and imparts its motion from one set of particles to another. Moreover, this air-motion is not, properly speaking, sound at all, but only gives rise to sensations of sound when it strikes upon the nervous mechanisms in our ears. If it were not for our ears, the violinists might draw their bows, and the trumpeters blow themselves breathless, and the drummers beat away for dear life, and there would be no sound at all—only a formidable atmospheric commotion.

But fortunately we have ears,—and ears capable of a most marvellous range, delicacy, and accuracy of hearing; and by their help we can pick out many different kinds of vibration in the air, and get from them as many different kinds of sensation. For example: pulsations of air that come irregularly, at varying periods of time, give us the sensation we call "noise"; pulsations that come at regular intervals we hear as "musical tones," and this in spite of the fact that they come so fast that we could not possibly count them, or even hear them individually (middle C, for example, is produced by no less than two hundred and fifty-six pulsations *per second*). The slower the puffs of air, the "lower" is the tone we hear, the more rapid the puffs, the "higher" the tone. The "lowest" tone we can hear is produced by about sixteen pulsations a second, the "highest" has about thirty-eight thousand—an almost inconceivable rapidity. Between these two extremes there are eleven thousand distinguishable tones, of which, however, we use only ninety in music. If the pulsations are weak, the tone is "soft"; if they are strong, it is "loud."

Furthermore, the ear is able to hear a whole series of pulsations, of varying rapidity, at once, and as constituting one "tone"—this tone, of course, being a compound of many simple tones which we fuse together. On this remarkable power depends our sense of differences in what we call "quality of tone," or *"timbre,"* and our ability to distinguish tones of the same pitch (*i. e.,* high or low position) played by different instruments such as a violin, a clarinet, an oboe, a trumpet. This is a matter so important to our understanding of the orchestra that it should be studied before we go farther.

Many of the elastic materials used to produce tones by their vibrations, as for instance a piano string, have the peculiarity of producing a whole series of vibrations, of varying rates of rapidity, at one and the same time. This depends on two facts: first, that the shorter the vibrating section of string the more rapid are its vibrations; second, that the piano string in question, when struck by the hammer, starts to vibrating not only *as a whole*, but also in segments of halves, thirds, quarters, fifths, sixths, sevenths, eighths, etc., of its entire length. Figure I. shows graphically these different modes of vibration, which for clearness we here represent separately, but which, it must be under-

THE NATURE OF SOUND

stood, actually take place simultaneously, hard as such a complicated kind of motion is for us to imagine.

FIGURE I.

EIGHT MODES OF VIBRATION IN A SINGLE STRING.

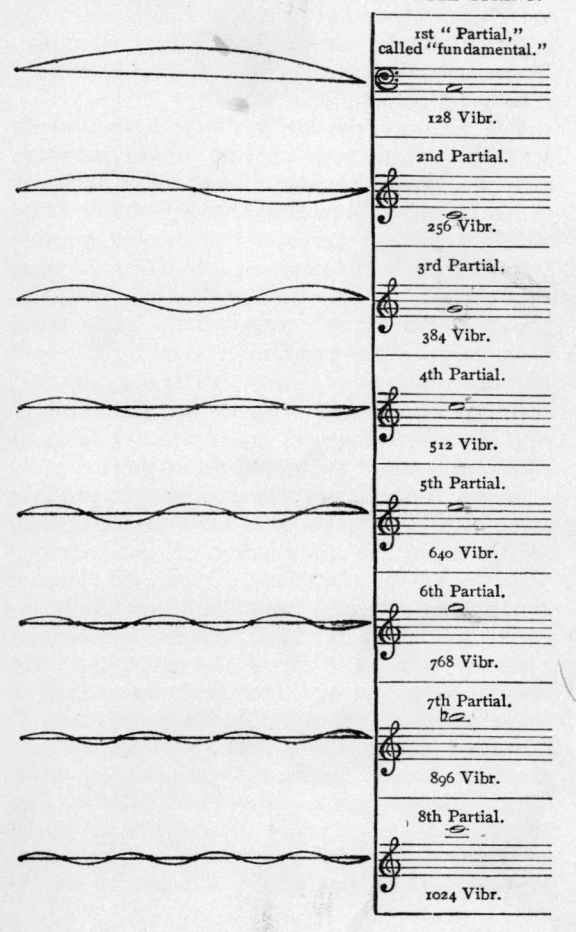

～	1st "Partial," called "fundamental." 128 Vibr.
～～	2nd Partial. 256 Vibr.
～～～	3rd Partial. 384 Vibr.
～～～～	4th Partial. 512 Vibr.
～～～～～	5th Partial. 640 Vibr.
～～～～～～	6th Partial. 768 Vibr.
～～～～～～～	7th Partial. 896 Vibr.
～～～～～～～～	8th Partial. 1024 Vibr.

The result of this peculiarity of our piano string is evidently that it gives forth, not a simple tone, as we are accustomed to think, but a whole series of "partial tones," as theorists call them. Let us suppose that the simplest mode of vibration, that of the string as a whole, produces 128 pulsations per second, as is actually the case with the piano string which gives forth the C an octave below middle C. Then the vibration by halves, occurring twice as fast, will give forth the tone middle C; the vibration by thirds, thrice as fast, will give forth the G above it; the vibration by fourths, four times as fast, will give forth the C above that; and so on. The whole series of "partial tones" up to the eighth, for this particular string, are shown in the column to the right, in Figure I, together with their vibration-rates per second.

But why, the reader will ask, do we not hear all these "partial" tones individually? There are two reasons. One is that the higher we go the fainter become the partial-tones, since the smaller the segment of the string the less is the amount or "amplitude" of the vibration, on which depends the loudness of the tone. (This is clearly shown in the figure.) Hence the first partial, the "fundamental tone," which is all we are ordinarily aware of hearing, is much louder and more prominent than any of the others. Indeed, although theoretically the partials continue *ad infinitum,* after the eighth they are so weak we need not consider them. The second reason is the overpowering influ-

THE NATURE OF SOUND

ence of habit. As all stringed instruments produce the whole series of partials together, we so habitually hear them all that we are unable to distinguish them one from another. With training, however, sensitive ears are able to pick out the first few partials easily and accurately.

But if we do not hear the partials as *quantity*, so to speak, we do, all of us, hear them as *quality;* for on them depends the peculiar *timbre* of each kind of tone. On account of mechanical differences, some instruments have more, or more prominent, upper partials than others. The general rule here is that the greater the number of partials the "richer," "fuller," more "brilliant" is the tone, as in the case of the violin; whereas the fewer, or fainter, the partials, the "purer," "quieter," "simpler" is the tone, as in the case of the lower tones of the flute, which have hardly any but the fundamental tones. The clarinet owes its individual quality to the fact that it has only the odd-numbered partials, the first, third, fifth, etc. The pungency of the tone of the oboe depends on its possessing high partials of considerable strength. Other instances of the effect of partial tones will meet us as we go on.

We have seen then, thus far, that all musical tones are produced by regularly periodic pulsations of the air, set up by the vibrations of elastic bodies, whether the strings of violins and the like, the air-columns of wind instruments, or the stretched membranes of drums or the metal of cymbals. We have seen that loudness depends on the force of these pulsations, and that pitch depends on their relative rapidity. Finally, we have seen that since almost every elastic body vibrates in a highly complex fashion, series of vibrations of more than one kind generally reach our ears from any one source; and that on the precise nature of these series depends what we call the *quality* of the particular tone.

II—CONSTITUTION OF THE ORCHESTRA.

The instruments used in the modern orchestra may be divided into three classes or families, according to the various modes in which their tones are produced. The most important group comprises the stringed instruments (often called simply "the Strings"), in which stretched strings are the vibrating bodies. The second group comprises the wind instruments ("the Wind"), in which the vibration arises in columns of air. The third group comprises the percussion instruments (sometimes called "the Battery"), in which stretched membranes or metallic bodies are the sources of vibration. These general groups may be further subdivided as shown in the following complete list of instruments, in which those seldom used in the orchestra are marked with asterisks. The figures in parenthesis show the number of each instrument used in the New York Symphony Orchestra.

CLASSIFIED LIST OF ORCHESTRAL INSTRUMENTS.
I—STRINGED INSTRUMENTS.

(*a*) Instruments played with a bow:
>Violin (34—18 1st violins, 16 2d violins)
>Viola (12).
>Violoncello (12).
>Double-bass (or contrabass), (10).

(*b*) Instruments the strings of which are plucked:
>Harp (1).
>*Guitar.
>*Mandoline.

(*c*) Instruments the strings of which are struck by hammers:
>*Pianoforte.

II—WIND INSTRUMENTS.

(*a*) Instruments sounded through a hole in the side of the tube:
>Flute (2).
>Piccolo (1).

(*b*) Instruments played with a double reed:
>Oboe (2).
>English Horn (or alto oboe), (1).
>Bassoon (3).
>*Contra-bassoon (or double bassoon), (1)

(*c*) Instruments played with a single reed:
>Clarinet (2).
>*Corno di bassetto.
>Bass Clarinet (1).
>*Saxophone.

(*d*) Instruments played with a mouthpiece:
>Trumpet (4).
>Cornet.

Horn (4).
Trombone (3).
*Ophicleide.
Tuba (1).

(e) Instruments with keyboards:
*Pipe organ.
*Reed organ.

III—PERCUSSION INSTRUMENTS.

(a) Tone produced by the vibration of a stretched membrane:
Kettle-drums (Timpani), (2).
*Bass drum, ⎫
*Side drum, ⎬ (4 players for other percussion instruments).
*Tambourine, ⎭

(b) Tone produced by the vibration of metallic bodies:
*Bells.
*Glockenspiel.
*Triangle.
Cymbals.
*Gong (Tam-tam).
*Castanets.

Summary of players in the New York Symphony Orchestra:

Strings	68
Harp	1
Wind	25
Percussion	5
	99

It must not be supposed, however, that this vast army of instruments is always, or even

CONSTITUTION OF THE ORCHESTRA

usually employed. Most of the important symphonic works of the nineteenth century can be performed by an orchestra made up as follows. (The instruments are put down in the order in which they occur in the full "score" from which the conductor reads):

Wood wind	2 Flutes, 1 interchangeable with piccolo. 2 Oboes. 2 Clarinets. 1 Bass Clarinet. 2 Bassoons. 1 Contrabassoon.
Brass and	4 Horns. 2 Trumpets. 3 Trombones. 1 Tuba.
Percussion	2 Kettle-drums.
Strings	First Violins. Second Violins. Violas. Violoncellos. Double-basses.

Some of the most imperishable symphonies call for even fewer instruments. Beethoven's Fifth Symphony, for example, requires no bass clarinet and no tuba, and only two horns. The lovely Andante of his Pastoral Symphony calls for only the following instruments, in addition to the usual strings: Two flutes, two oboes, two clarinets, two bassoons, and two horns. This modest combination, called the "small orchestra" (distinguished from the "grand orchestra" by lacking trumpets and drums), is also used by him in the Larghetto of the Second

Symphony and in the Allegretto of the Eighth. It has also been used most effectively by some modern composers, as for instance by Dvořák in his charming Suite for Small Orchestra, Opus 39.

The modern tendency, on the other hand, initiated by Berlioz and fostered by Liszt and Wagner, has been constantly to increase the number and variety of the instruments. Wagner, in "Die Walküre," besides the usual strings, calls for two piccolos, two flutes, three oboes, one English horn, three clarinets, one bass clarinet, three bassoons, eight horns, four trumpets, one bass trumpet, four trombones, one to four tubas, two pairs of kettle-drums, one pair of cymbals, one bass-drum, and six harps. Berlioz had what amounted almost to a mania for monster orchestras. In his Requiem we find him prescribing sixteen trombones, sixteen trumpets, five ophicleides, twelve horns, eight pairs of kettle-drums, two bass-drums, and a gong, in addition to the usual resources. "Prince Metternich," he tells us in his Memoirs, "said to me one day: 'Are you not the man, monsieur, who composes music for five hundred performers?' To which I replied: 'Not always, monseigneur; I sometimes write for four hundred and fifty.'"

III—A BIRD'S-EYE VIEW OF THE ORCHESTRA.

Let us now take a general look at the orchestra and its arrangement on the stage, before we examine in more detail the separate instruments.

of the stage. The instruments, of polished brass, the tube made into a circle with its very flaring mouth facing sideways, are not hard to identify. The trumpets, looking not unlike large cornets, are near them. On the outer edge of the orchestra, at the right, are the trombones, recognizable by their slides, which the players draw in and out to shorten or lengthen the tubes. And that enormous brass instrument which seems as if it would drag the poor player to the ground by its sheer weight, and which is evidently most exhausting to play, what is that? It is the tuba, the bass of the trombones.

Finally, there are the kettle-drums, at the very back, between the tuba-trombone group and the last of the double-basses, and sometimes, next them, the great bass-drum and the brazen cymbals.

CHAPTER II.

IV—THE STRINGED INSTRUMENTS.

The choir of stringed instruments, consisting of first violins, second violins, violas, violoncellos, and double-basses, is by far the most important single department of the orchestra.

The reasons for its supremacy are many. In the first place, it commands a greater range of tones than any other group, covering no less than six octaves. Secondly, its facility of execution is greater. Violins and violas, and even violoncellos, can play at almost any rate of speed, and can produce with perfect clearness the most complicated runs and passages; and unlike the wind instruments they can hold a single tone as long as may be desired. In the third place, the strings can play with any degree of force from the boldest fortissimo to the merest breath of pianissimo. The wind instruments cannot command anything like such a delicate immateriality of tone, and when they come in on the final chord of a piece ending very softly often give the hearer a slight shock.

Bowed instruments, furthermore, can be played for any length of time without fatiguing the performer, while the wind instrument players must have frequent rests to regain their breath and to relax the muscles which, in playing such instruments as the horn, have to be contracted in a way that soon becomes wearisome.

FIRST VIOLIN

The hearer, too, can stand more string-tone than wind-tone. The peculiar *timbre* of such instruments as the oboe, the clarinet, the trumpet, would grow cloying if we had to listen to it for long stretches of time; the full, round, and yet simple tone of the violins is better suited to be "human nature's daily food."

For all these reasons the strings are the nucleus of the orchestra. They may, for the sake of contrast, give way to the other instruments for short periods, but they are never silent very long, and they are themselves capable of remarkable variety without any outside help.

V.—THE VIOLIN.

The violin has four strings, tuned as follows:

FIGURE III.

TUNING AND RANGE OF THE VIOLIN.

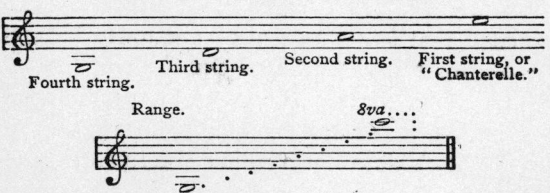

Fourth string. Third string. Second string. First string, or "Chanterelle."

Range. *8va*....

They are tuned by pegs set in the neck of the instrument, are pressed by the fingers of the left hand to change their pitch (this is called "stopping"), and are set in vibration by the bow being drawn across them by the right hand. Only a small portion of the tone comes, however, from the strings themselves. The vibrations are carried from them, through the bridge, into the wooden body of the violin, which is so delicately made as to vibrate in "sympathy," producing the larger portion of the sound. The extraordinary sonority of the instrument is due to this delicacy of construction.

The bridge over which the strings pass is arched in such a way that the bow can touch any one string without coming in contact with the others. This serves very well with a slight pressure such as is used in soft passages; but it is impossible to play heavily on the two middle strings, the D and the A strings, without touching adjacent strings. For this reason it will be found that fortissimo passages generally lie chiefly on the E or the G string. Indeed, the first string (E-string) is used so preponderantly for melody that it is often called the "chanterelle," or "singer." It has been calculated that two-thirds of all the tones Mozart wrote for the violin lie on the E-string.

The tone of this string has a peculiar incisiveness, a penetrating quality that makes it easily heard above everything else in fortissimo passages for the full orchestra; in pianissimo it is wonderfully clear, pure, ethereal. Whether loud or soft, it stands in relief above the other orchestral sounds like a thread of scarlet in a mass of duller hues.

No small part of the effectiveness of Weber's orchestration, in his famous overtures, "Euryanthe" and "Oberon," is due to his use of the

THE VIOLIN
FIGURE IV.

Allegro con fuoco.   WEBER: "Oberon."

Allegro, molto appassionato.   MENDELSSOHN: Concerto for Violin.

E-string. An example is shown in Figure IV, (*a*). For softer but not less thrilling effects we may turn to Mendelssohn, whose delicate, aristocratic nature made him sensitive to the beautiful clarity of this tone. (*b*), in Figure IV, shows the opening theme of his Violin Concerto, lying entirely on the E-string.

The second or A-string, and even more the third or D-string, are quieter and paler than the chanterelle. Nevertheless they are capable of very lovely effects, of which Schumann has made use in the slow movement of his second symphony, and Beethoven in the mystical Adagio of the Ninth Symphony (Figure V).

FIGURE V.

Adagio espressivo. SCHUMANN: Symphony II.

Adagio molto e cantabile. BEETHOVEN: Symphony IX.

The fourth or G-string is not only thicker than all the others, but is wound with wire to make it heavier and therefore slower in vibration. The result is a remarkable fulness of tone, like that of a rich contralto voice. In expression it is intense, earnest, impassioned. We are all familiar with those moments when the players, bending their heads close to their violins as if caressing them, raise their bow-arms well up to get a free sweep across the G-string. This effect, like all good things, may be abused, and every trivial "Romance for Violin" has its solo for the fourth string. But if the melody itself has nobility, it can gain through the massive sonority of this string an almost overpowering intensity of expressiveness, especially when rendered by a large number of instruments, as will be realized by referring to the examples in Figure VI.

THE VIEW VIOLIN

FIGURE VI.

(a) *Adagio.*   WAGNER: "Lohengrin."

(b) *Sostenuto assai.*   WAGNER: "Tannhäuser."

(c) *Adagio assai,*   BEETHOVEN: Funeral March, from Symphony III.

(d) *Adagio assai.*   Ibid.

Chords of two, three, or four tones may be produced on the violin by sweeping the bow across several strings. A sustained tone cannot be attained, however, on more than two strings at once, on account of the arched shape of the bridge already mentioned. This process of playing chords of two tones, on two strings, is called double-stopping, because the left hand has to press or "stop" two strings at once. In orchestral music only the easiest chords of this kind are written, since the desired effect of full harmony can be better obtained by dividing the violins into two or more groups, letting each play one of the desired tones. The indication for this is the Italian word "divisi."

Great diversity of expression is possible to the violin through the various methods of bowing or phrasing. When a series of tones is played by one movement of the bow (indicated by putting a slur over them—see Figures IV-VI), we get a smooth *legato,* or "bound together" effect, such as we get with the voice when many tones are sung for one syllable. When each tone is given by a separate bow-stroke the effect is of animation, energy, or grandiloquence. A peculiar delicacy is gained, in rapid tempos, by the use of the "arco saltando" or "flying bow," *i. e.,* the bow allowed to leap up from the string by its own elasticity.

The "tremolo" is made by moving the bow back and forth with great rapidity on the same string or pair of strings, and has a mysterious, menacing, or exciting quality. Like the G-string solo, it is easily abused: in the theatrical melodrama the approach of the villain is usually accompanied by a tremolo of all the strings. This device is skilfully used by Weber in the introduction to his "Freischütz" overture.

Instead of being bowed, the strings may be plucked by the finger. This is called the "pizzicato"—Italian for "plucked." The pizzicato is generally used either to gain a certain incisiveness like that of the percussion instruments, or to make the tone more delicate and immaterial. It is oftener used in accompaniments by the lower strings, or for the bass, than by the first violin. Schubert makes use of pizzicato in the violins, violas and double-basses, to accompany a solo by the 'cellos, later joined by the oboe, in a well-known passage in the Andante of his C-major Symphony (Figure VII).

FIGURE VII.

In his fourth symphony Tschaikowsky makes striking use of the pizzicato of all the strings throughout the scherzo.

The "mute," or "sordino," is a little metal

clamp which, when placed upon the bridge, impedes the transmission of the vibrations into the body of the violin, thus making the tone not only softer, but different in quality—thin, veiled, mysterious. Gounod has made use of this peculiar quality of tone in the scene of Marguerite's hallucination in prison, in his "Faust," and Beethoven has used it, in the third act of "Fidelio," for the scene between Leonore and the jailer. Tschaikowsky uses it with great impressiveness at the end of his great "Symphonie Pathetique." (See also Figures XII and XIII *a*.)

By placing his finger lightly on the middle of one of the strings, or at the point marking exactly one third, one fourth, one fifth of it, etc., the violinist can make it vibrate in certain segments only, instead of as a whole, thus producing only certain "partial tones" or "harmonics" (see Figure I, and the explanation in Section I of the mode of vibration of a string). These harmonics have a peculiar thinness and purity of tone, and may be most tellingly used in the orchestra. Wagner thus uses the high ghostly harmonics of four solo violins at the beginning of his "Lohengrin" Prelude.

There are certain other peculiar effects obtainable by special ways of playing the violin and the other stringed instruments, such for example as the "col legno" (touching the strings with the back of the bow instead of with the hairs), but those we have already mentioned are the most important. They are all applicable to the entire group of stringed instruments, though harmonics and the mute or sordino are seldom used on the double-bass.

A word must be said here as to the second violins, the group of players immediately to the right of the conductor, at the front of the stage. They play, of course, exactly the same kind of instrument as the first violins, and are to be distinguished from them merely by the different functions they are called upon to perform. While the first violins often carry the main melody, the seconds much less frequently do so, but generally fill up one of the harmonic "parts." When the firsts have a melody lying high up on the E-string, however, the seconds often reënforce them by playing the same melody an octave lower. Figures so rapid as to present great difficulties to the players are also sometimes divided between the two, the firsts playing only a few measures and then being relieved by the seconds. In "tuttis" (an Italian word meaning "all," and indicating those passages, generally loud, where all the orchestra is employed together), the seconds often join the firsts, the lower parts of the harmony being entrusted to other instruments.

VI.—THE VIOLA.

The viola, in appearance exactly like the violin save for its slightly greater size, is the alto of the string choir, and is indeed by the French called the "Alto." In Germany it is known as the "Bratsche" (Brah-tcha). Its

FIGURE VIII.

TUNING AND RANGE OF THE VIOLA.

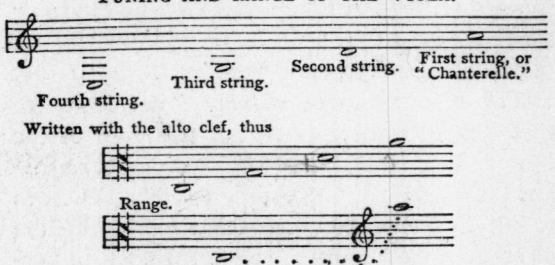

Fourth string. Third string. Second string. First string, or "Chanterelle."

Written with the alto clef, thus

Range.

four strings are tuned a fifth lower than those of the violin (see Figure VIII), and music for it is written in the so-called alto clef which puts middle C on the third line.

The quality of tone of the viola differs considerably from that of the violin, on account of the different proportion between the length and the thickness of the strings. The viola strings are much thicker and heavier in proportion to their length, and hence have a less brilliant but in some respects a richer tone. There is a certain sinister, austere, dark quality about the viola tone which is characteristic, and which adds a valuable pigment to the composer's palette.

The viola, however, is seldom used as a solo instrument in the orchestra. Its most usual functions are the following: (1) to take one of the lower strands of the harmony, generally what corresponds to the tenor part in a chorus; (2) to double the first or second violins or some other solo instrument in melodies; (3) to pro-

'CELLO

THE VIOLONCELLO

vide the bass in soft, delicate combinations when the lower stringed instruments are silent or being otherwise used.

VII.—THE VIOLONCELLO.

The violoncello, the large stringed instrument held between the knees of the player, has four strings much longer than those of the viola, and tuned an octave lower (see Figure IX). It is an instrument of remarkable versatility, though undoubtedly its most frequent use is to supply the bass, either with or without the double-bass, which usually plays an octave lower.

FIGURE IX.

TUNING AND RANGE OF THE VIOLONCELLO.

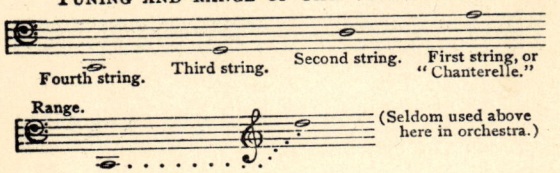

Fourth string.   Third string.   Second string.   First string, or "Chanterelle."

Range.   (Seldom used above here in orchestra.)

The peculiarly full, rich tone of the 'cello, however, especially of its "chanterelle" or A-string, makes it an admirable solo instrument, to which many of the most inspired melodies in orchestral music owe much of their eloquence. How unforgettable is the lovely second theme of the first movement of Schubert's Unfinished Symphony, sung by the 'cellos against a throbbing accompaniment of the violas and clarinets![1] (See Figure X, *a*). Not less deserved-

---

[1] The 'cello solo in Figure VII., from Schubert, is also worthy of note. It lies entirely on the A-string.

FIGURE X.

(a) Allegro moderato.   SCHUBERT: Unfinished Symphony.

(b) Andante con moto.   BEETHOVEN: Fifth Symphony.

ly famous is the theme of the Andante of Beethoven's Fifth Symphony, in which the 'cellos are joined by the violas (Figure X, *b*). A more modern example is the chief melody of Goldmark's overture, "Sakuntala." Here the richness of the 'cello tone is enhanced by the addition of a clarinet in its low register (Figure XI).

FIGURE XI.

Moderato assai.   GOLDMARK: "Sakuntala" Overture.

THE VIOLONCELLO

In his "Pathetic Symphony," Tschaikowsky assigns the first entrance of the suave second theme to the first violins and the violoncellos, playing an octave apart, and with mutes (sordini), (Figure XII). The accompaniment is supplied almost entirely by wind instruments (horns, clarinets, and bassoons), against which the string tone stands out in strong relief.

FIGURE XII.

TSCHAIKOWSKY: Pathetic Symphony.

34 THE ORCHESTRAL INSTRUMENTS

Owing to this prominent relief in which the tone of the 'cello A-string always stands out, the 'cello is often written above the viola when it is desired to emphasize an important part in the middle of the orchestral web. In nothing, perhaps, is the skill of the adept orchestrator more subtly shown than in these fine bits of coloring which a careless or inexperienced reader of the score easily misses altogether. At the beginning of that little masterpiece, the Adagietto of Bizet's "L'Arlesienne" Suite, intended to accompany the meeting of the old lovers in the drama, and scored for muted violins, violas, and 'cellos alone, Bizet gives the bass to the violas, saving the 'cellos for the more expressive tenor voice (see Figure XIII,

FIGURE XIII.

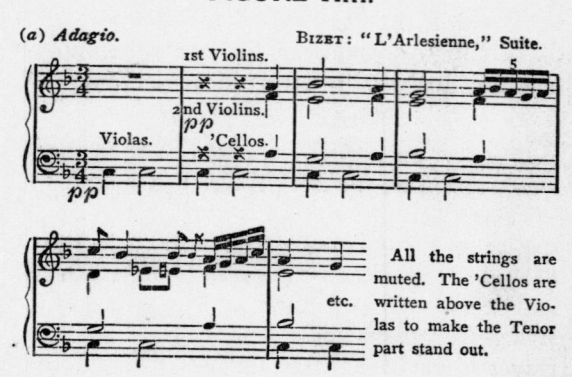

(a) *Adagio.* BIZET: "L'Arlesienne," Suite.

All the strings are muted. The 'Cellos are written above the Violas to make the Tenor part stand out.

(b) *Allegro molto.*   Dvořák: "New World" Symphony.

This is simplified for piano. In the orchestral version the 'cellos take the half-notes, while the violas fill up the harmony below them.

a). Were the instruments reversed the beautiful passage would lose much of its color. Again, in a memorable passage in the "New World" Symphony (Figure XIII, *b*), Dvořák brings his violoncellos up above his violas for a few measures, simply to get their mordant, penetrating tone on that wonderful C-sharp in the fourth measure of our excerpt, which no one who has heard it is likely to forget.

Did space permit, many examples of this kind of subtlety in orchestral coloring might be studied. It may be said in passing that the help which the reading of orchestral scores gives to the appreciation of just such elusive beauties is one of its greatest advantages.

VIII.—THE DOUBLE-BASS.

It is the business of this bulky instrument, well nicknamed the "bull fiddle," to sustain the bass part, either with or without the help of the 'cello, the bassoon, or the tuba. Owing to the great length and thickness of its strings it is incapable of such rapid figures as the other stringed instruments. The fingers have to traverse so much space that it is found convenient to tune the strings in smaller inter-

36 THE ORCHESTRAL INSTRUMENTS

vals than on the 'cello (in fourths instead of fifths). (See Figure XIV).

FIGURE XIV.

TUNING AND RANGE OF THE DOUBLEBASS.

Fourth string. Third string. Second string. First string.

Range (actual sounds): (Seldom used above here.)

The part for the double-bass in the orchestral score is written an octave higher than it sounds. This is the first instance we have met with of a "transposing instrument," that is, an instrument which plays tones different from those written on the score. Transposing instruments are of several kinds, and the transpositions, as we shall later see, are introduced for various purposes. In the present instance there are two reasons. It used to be customary for the double-basses to play from the violoncello parts, one double-bass and one 'cello playing at each desk. The double-bass in this case always played an octave below the 'cello. This custom has become obsolete, but its influence on the notation remains.

The second reason why the double-bass part is written an octave higher than it sounds is that this method brings practically all its notes on the staff. If it were written where it

DOUBLEBASS

sounds, great inconvenience to the copyist would result from the many leger lines that would have to be used.

Before the time of Beethoven the doublebass was a humdrum instrument, invaluable to the ensemble but possessing little individuality. Beethoven, with his characteristic independence, used it for special effects, making it humorous in the scherzo of the Fifth Symphony (Figure XV, *a*) and notably eloquent in the famous recitatives of the Ninth Symphony.

FIGURE XV.

(*a*) *Allegro.*   BEETHOVEN: Fifth Symphony.
Double Basses and Violoncellos.

(*b*) *Adagio.*   TSCHAIKOWSKY: Symphonie Pathetique.
Doublebasses divided. Bassoon.
Violas divided.

(*c*) *Molto adagio.*   DVOŘÁK: "New World" Symphony.
Violins, Violas, and 'Cellos.
Doublebasses divided in four groups.

38 THE ORCHESTRAL INSTRUMENTS

In our own day it has been used with daring originality by Tschaikowsky and others, who sometimes divide the double-basses into several groups. Thus the memorable opening of the "Pathetic Symphony" is scored for double-basses in two divisions and bassoons in their low register—a most mysterious effect. (Figure XV, *b*). Dvořák, at the end of the slow movement of his "New World" Symphony, writes a chord for double-basses alone, in four groups, one for each tone. (Figure XV, *c*). One also finds in modern scores the double-basses sometimes written above the violoncellos, when the composer has some especial design in view.

The harp, although not a regular member of the orchestral forces, deserves a word here. It has forty-six strings, tuned to the diatonic scale of C-flat, but fastened to pedals operated by the feet, by which they can be so tightened that all keys are available. The plucking of the strings by the fingers gives a certain not unpleasant twang characteristic of the instrument. It is chiefly used in accompaniment, sounding chords and arpeggios (the latter word being, by the way, derived from its Italian name).

The "harmonics" of the harp, wondrously clear and ethereal, have been cleverly used by Berlioz in his "Dance of Sylphs."

HARP

CHAPTER III.

IX.—THE WOOD-WIND INSTRUMENTS.

The second important division of the orchestra, after the strings, is the choir of wood-wind instruments, namely flutes, oboes, clarinets, and bassoons, to which are sometimes added the kindred instruments, piccolo, English horn, bass clarinet, and contra-bassoon.[1]

This division is much less homogeneous, and much less frequently used *en masse*, than that of the strings; there is far more difference between flutes and oboes, for example, than there is between violins and violas or 'cellos. Moreover, the wood-wind instruments, as was stated above, are both more fatiguing to play for long stretches, and more monotonous in their effect upon the listener, than the strings. Hence they are used chiefly for contrast and color, either as solo instruments or for intensifying particular strands in the web of tone. From such employment of them, skilfully made, there result a hundred shades and half-shades of color as delicate as the iridescent hues of a seashell.

In all wind instruments (brass as well as wood) the tone is produced by the vibration

---

(1) The horns, not to be confused with the English horn, which is an instrument of the oboe family, are sometimes grouped with the wood-wind, although made of brass, because their tone is so soft and mellow that it merges well with wood tone and is often used with it. We shall, however, for simplicity, not take up the horns until after we have treated the wood-wind.

of columns of air rather than by that of strings and their wooden supports, as in the string instruments. The differences in the tone qualities and modes of playing the wind instruments arise from differing methods of starting such vibration (direct blowing in the flute, a double-reed in oboes and bassoons, a single reed in clarinets, etc.), and from differing ways of altering the pitch.

In order to understand the latter point, alteration of pitch, it is necessary to bear constantly in mind two general principles. First, other things being equal, the longer the column of air the slower will be its vibration, and consequently the lower will be the tone it emits. Second, a column of air, like a string, can vibrate either as a whole, or in segments of one-half its length, one-third its length, one-fourth its length, etc., or in several of these ways at once. Each of these modes of vibration gives rise to its own "partial" tone, and on the number and relative strength of the various partials depends the peculiar *timbre* or tone-color characteristic of each instrument.

If these facts are borne in mind the reader will easily grasp the principles of construction of the various wind instruments.

X.—THE FLUTE.

The flute is easily identified at sight in the orchestra as the only instrument which the player blows *across* instead of directly into. Made either of wood or of metal, it is provided with keys which when pressed by the fingers open holes in the tube, thus altering the pitch by shortening the vibratory column

FLUTE

of air. In this way are obtained all the tones from middle C to the C-sharp an octave above it (See Figure XVI), these tones being produced by the vibration of the air column as a whole.

FIGURE XVI.

RANGE AND QUALITIES OF THE FLUTE.

First register, produced by low pressure: Woody, dark, menacing.

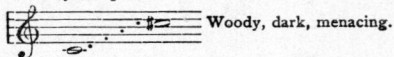

Second register, produced by increased pressure: Clear, mellow, "flutey."

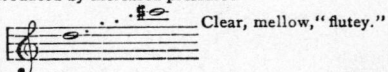

Third register, produced by still greater pressure: Bright, brilliant.

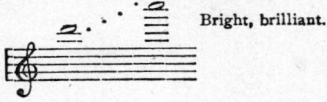

The higher registers, also shown in Figure XVI, are obtained by simply *blowing harder* (with certain changes of fingering), which causes the air column to break up and vibrate in sections instead of as a whole. This increased wind pressure produces the *second partial,* an octave higher than the fundamental tone, which gives, with the help of the holes and keys in altering the length of the air column, another group of tones an octave higher than the first. Still greater pressure produces the *third partial,* an octave and a fifth higher than the first or fundamental tone, and so on. The higher registers are keener and more penetrating in quality than the lower, the extreme upper tones being most brilliant. The char-

42 THE ORCHESTRAL INSTRUMENTS

acteristic qualities of the different registers are indicated in the figure.

The flute is most frequently used as a solo instrument in light, delicate, lyrical passages. The classical instance, often quoted but never hackneyed, is the filmy scherzo in the "Midsummer Night's Dream" music of Mendelssohn, a composer whose fanciful genius has used the flute with incomparable felicity (Figure XVII).

FIGURE XVII.

MENDELSSOHN: Scherzo, "Midsummer Night's Dream."

THE FLUTE

The flute here plays a rapid figure in sixteenth notes, at first supported by chords for the strings, later all alone so that it is heard to great advantage. Beginning this part in its "woody" lower register, it gradually climbs up into brighter regions until, at the return of the main melody, the best tones of the flute are heard in dainty two-part harmony.

FIGURE XVIII.

44   THE ORCHESTRAL INSTRUMENTS

etc.

Figure XVIII, from Bizet, shows a different use of two flutes together. Here the tones are sustained, melodious, instead of delicately staccato, and the style and rhythm of the music are pastoral. The momentary dissonance caused by the first flute taking B-natural against the second flute's B-sharp is a point of special beauty. Later the two oboes join in, lending with their more pungent tone additional force to the same dissonance (F-sharp against F-double-sharp).

FIGURE XIX.

Andante con moto. MENDELSSOHN: Italian Symphony.

(The stems of the notes for the violins are turned upwards, those of the notes for the flutes downwards.)

In the passage from Mendelssohn's Italian Symphony, shown in Figure XIX, the flutes merely provide an accompaniment to the violin melody—but an accompaniment of what deliciously melting harmony! No one who has heard this passage is likely to forget its ravishing beauty, produced by surprisingly simple means.

In forte and fortissimo passages for the full orchestra ("tutti") the two flutes are ordinarily either placed with the violins on the melody or given holding chords with the other instruments of their family.

The piccolo is a small flute playing an octave higher than the ordinary instrument, and used chiefly to give additional brightness to "tutti" passages, as at the end of Beethoven's "Egmont" Overture. The notes for it are written an octave lower than they sound.

XI.—THE OBOE.

The oboe differs from the flute in that the column of air within its tube is set in motion not directly, but through the medium of a double-reed, consisting of two thin slips of cane set against each other so as to leave a passage for the air, and placed in the mouthpiece of the instrument. This mode of starting the vibration, producing as it does a tone containing several "upper partials," is the reason for the peculiar "reedy," almost querulous quality of the oboe tone. As in the flute, the changes of pitch are produced in part by a mechanism of holes and keys, in part by variations of breath-pressure. The range and qualities of the oboe are shown in Figure XX.

FIGURE XX.

RANGE AND QUALITIES OF THE OBOE.

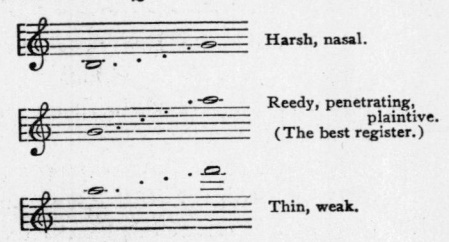

Harsh, nasal.

Reedy, penetrating, plaintive.
(The best register.)

Thin, weak.

It is a peculiarity of the oboe that the wind-pressure has to be very light, so light indeed that the player can never fully empty his lungs. For this reason he soon becomes fatigued, and rests have to be given him frequently.

In common with the other double-reed instruments, the English horn, the bassoon, and the double-bassoon, and with single-reed instruments such as the clarinet, the oboe has a much more expressive tone, and a greater range of power between pianissimo and fortissimo, than the flute, and adapts itself consequently to a greater diversity of uses in the orchestra. It is much more used as a solo instrument, however, than in any other way, as its tone is so penetrating that it cannot easily be subordinated to anything else.

OBOE

THE OBOE

FIGURE XXI.

Allegro.   Beethoven: Pastoral Symphony.

Beethoven had a great fondness for the oboe, and his scores abound in oboe solos of the most varied character, always effect ve. He frequently avails himself of the half-humorous, half-tender qualities of the oboe in staccato or tripping utterance, as for example in the melody from the scherzo of the Pastoral Symphony shown above. On the other hand, no one knew better its capacities for serious expression. In the great Funeral March of his "Eroica" Symphony, after announcing his theme on the G-string of the violins (as shown in Figure VI, *c*), he answers them, with poignant beauty, by the thinner, slighter, yet infinitely plaintive tones of the oboe (Figure XXII).

FIGURE XXII.

Adagio assai.   Beethoven: Eroica Symphony.

cresc. decresc.   *p*

48 THE ORCHESTRAL INSTRUMENTS

FIGURE XXIII.

A remarkably imaginative treatment of the oboe is Schubert's in the slow movement of his Unfinished Symphony (Figure XXIII)—

THE OBOE

a treatment in which the appropriate use of the instrument is enhanced by harmonic ingenuities. Against gently pulsing chords in the strings the oboe outlines a quiet, sad melody, which soon becomes agitated and reaches the high F with an almost passionate intensity. Here it rests for three measures, sinking back by delicate gradations to *piano,* while the harmony similarly lapses from the key of B-flat, through the minor, to that of D-flat. The final E of the oboe is another instance of those long-held notes, gradually dying away, which it renders so incomparably.

FIGURE XXIV.

Largo. DVOŘÁK: "New World" Symphony.

Though used infrequently for anything but melody, oboe-tone is sometimes just what is wanted to give saliency, depth, or richness to some minor strand of the harmony. The example from Dvořák (Figure XXIV) illustrates this sort of case. Here two oboes are used as an accompaniment to a somber melody given to the clarinet—a combination as novel as it is happy. The profound melancholy of both theme and tone-color in this beautiful passage make it one of the finest things in modern musical literature.

The English horn, misleadingly named, is in reality not a horn at all, but a larger and lower-pitched oboe. It is indeed the alto of the oboe family, bearing much the relation to the ordinary oboe that the viola bears to the violin. Its tube is half as long again as that of the oboe, and its pitch and range a fifth lower. It is a transposing instrument, the music for it being written a fifth higher than it sounds.

In the English horn the richness and expressiveness of oboe tone are enhanced by the lower pitch, so that it is one of the most eloquent of solo instruments for melodies of a melancholy or exotic character. It has never been used to better purpose than by Dvořák in the symphony from which we have already quoted so often—in the slow movement, of which it announces the theme:—

ENGLISH HORN

THE ENGLISH HORN

FIGURE XXV.

It is also finely used by Goldmark in his "Sakuntala" Overture, where he assigns to it and the oboe, in octaves, the languorous second theme:

FIGURE XXVI.

At the end of the "Scene in the Fields" in his "Symphonie Fantastique," Berlioz has given fragments of his theme to the English horn, accompanied only by four kettle-drums, pianissimo. Of this passage he himself remarks, in his treatise on Orchestration: "The feelings of absence, of forgetfulness, of sorrowful loneliness, which arise in the bosoms of the audience on hearing this forsaken melody would lack half their power if played by any other instrument than the English horn."

XII.—THE CLARINET.

The clarinet, perhaps the most useful of all wood-wind instruments on account of its great range, its beautiful quality, and its facility of execution as regards both speed and variation of force, differs mechanically from the oboe, which it closely resembles in appearance, in two important respects. It is played not by a double but by a single reed, which is pressed against the player's lower lip, and its tube is cylindrical instead of conical.

A curious result of this construction is that the *evenly numbered partial tones,* the second, fourth, sixth, etc., are not produced, and the presence of only the odd partials in the tone give it a most individual coloring. This absence of the useful second partial tone, which gives flute and oboe their second octave, also produces inequalities of tone in the different registers, and necessitates irregularities of fingering.

Three different clarinets are in use in the orchestra, identical as to holes, keys, and fingering, but differing in length, and consequently in pitch. These are the clarinet in C, the clari-

CLARINET

THE CLARINET

net in B-flat, and the clarinet in A, commonly called "C clarinet," "B clarinet," and "A clarinet." Of these the C clarinet, on account of its slightly inferior tone-quality, is least used; but as it is the type of all clarinets it must be described first.

The full length of the tube of the C clarinet, with low breath-pressure, sounds the E below middle C. With the same breath-pressure, the player obtains by the use of the keys all the tones up to the E just above middle C. This register is called the "Chalumeau" (see Figure XXVII), and is of a wondrous mellowness and richness of tone.

FIGURE XXVII.

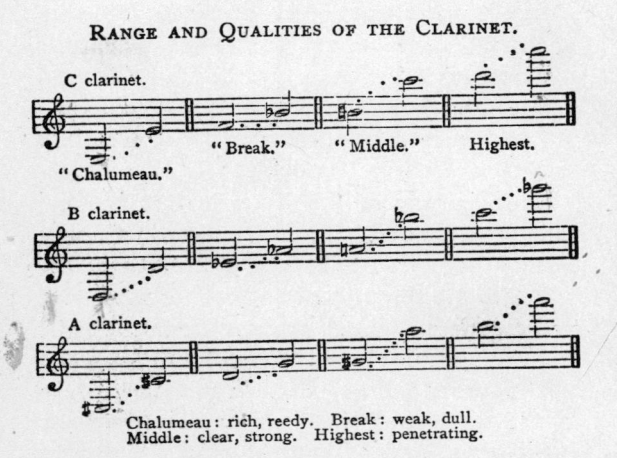

RANGE AND QUALITIES OF THE CLARINET.

Chalumeau: rich, reedy. Break: weak, dull.
Middle: clear, strong. Highest: penetrating.

As the second partial cannot be sounded, however, the next tone obtainable by increase of pressure is the *third* partial of the original low E, which is the B above middle C. From the chalumeau to this B, therefore, extends the so-called "Break" in the instrument, of which the tones are produced by extra keys, and are of inferior quality. They are also difficult to produce rapidly. This break is the most unfortunate feature of the clarinet, and, as we shall presently see, is one of the chief reasons why it is desirable to use clarinets of varying pitch.

The register produced by the third partial tones (altered in pitch, of course, by the keys) extends for about an octave above the B above middle C, and is called the middle register. This is of a fine clarity and nobility of tone. Above it extends the highest register of the instrument, useful though less brilliant than the same tones of the flute, and produced by still greater breath-pressure, with certain complexities of fingering into which it is not necessary to enter.

The registers of the B clarinet correspond exactly to those of the instrument in C, save that on account of the greater length of the tube they are throughout a major second lower. The registers of the A clarinet are in the same way a minor third lower. (See Figure XXVII).

The reader will now ask, Why is it necessary to use these other instruments at all? Why cannot one kind of clarinet play all clarinet music?

The reason is, first, that music written in keys in which there are many sharps or flats involves great difficulties in fingering, which may become almost insuperable in complicated passages, but which are easily evaded by using a differently tuned instrument. For example, suppose we are writing in the key of F-sharp, which has six sharps. If we were to use C clarinets the players would throw up their hands in despair at so many sharps, and very likely declare their parts unplayable. If, however, we should use B clarinets, which produce tones a major second lower than those written, we should be able to write their part in the key of A-flat (a major second higher than F-sharp) which would give them only four flats; and flats, moreover, are easier for wind instruments than sharps. Or we could use A clarinets, writing them in the key of A, which has but three sharps. Since the A clarinet sounds a minor third lower than written, this would bring them where we want them.

In short, like all transposing instruments the B and A clarinets are used when and where their parts will be easiest and most effective, the composer remembering that a B clarinet will sound a major second or whole step lower than it is written, an A clarinet a minor third, or step and a half, lower.

A further reason for the practice, in the case of the clarinets, is the "Break." Suppose we want the notes lying just at the upper edge of the "break" in the C clarinet: we can get them in a good quality of tone and with no difficulties for the player by simply changing to

56 THE ORCHESTRAL INSTRUMENTS

an A clarinet, on which these same tones lie in the excellent middle register.

("The clarinet," says Berlioz, "is an epic instrument. Its voice is that of heroic love. The character of the sounds of the medium register, imbued with a kind of loftiness tempering a noble tenderness, render them favorable for the expression of sentiments and ideas the most poetic.") This lofty and impassioned tenderness of the clarinet is splendidly utilized in the solo from the "Freischütz" Overture of Weber, a composer who made the clarinet peculiarly his own, shown in Figure XXVIII, *a*. The long

FIGURE XXVIII.

(a) Molto vivace.   Weber: "Freischütz" Overture.

Con molto passione.

(b) Allegretto.   Beethoven: Seventh Symphony.

dolce.

THE CLARINET

(c) Allegro, grazioso.   BRAHMS: Third Symphony.

notes of the clarinet here, against an exciting tremolo of the accompanying strings, are most impressive.

The second example in the same figure is a melody from Beethoven's Seventh Symphony, in which the middle register is used for a quieter and more lyrical expression, while in Figure XXVIII, *c* we have a more modern example, a theme from Brahms, in which the clarinet becomes appealing, almost plaintive.

58 THE ORCHESTRAL INSTRUMENTS

The lower notes given to the right hand in this piano version are carried by the bassoon, the tone of which merges perfectly with that of the clarinet.

It is less frequently that we find the clarinet used for gay pastoral tunes, for which the flute and the oboe are better suited; nevertheless Mendelssohn thus uses it, most successfully, in the jig-like Scherzo of his Scotch Symphony, as shown in Figure XXIX.

FIGURE XXIX.

Vivace non troppo. MENDELSSOHN: Scotch Symphony.

The tone of the chalumeau register is highly individual—rich and mellow, yet with a certain somberness. Weber was the first to appreciate fully its possibilities for dramatic expression, and the example he set has been followed by many modern composers. Thus Tschaikowsky, for example, opens his Fifth Symphony with a mournful theme allotted to two clarinets in unison, in the chalumeau register, accompanied by the low strings: (Figure XXX). This register can be used for accompaniment as effectively as for melodies, since the individuality of the tone is sufficiently strong to color the whole combination. The

BASS CLARINET

THE CLARINET

passage from Dvořák shown in Figure XXIV, is soon repeated, an octave lower, the oboes replaced by the clarinets (chalumeau) and the melody assigned to the G-string of the first violins—a combination of remarkable sonority.

FIGURE XXX.

TSCHAIKOWSKY: Fifth Symphony.

The bass clarinet, of comparatively recent introduction into the orchestra, is much larger than the ordinary instrument, and sounds an octave lower. As in the case of the ordinary clarinet, two forms are in use, one in B-flat and one in A. The quality of tone is rich, like the chalumeau of the other clarinets, and the instrument can be used either for solo or for

60 THE ORCHESTRAL INSTRUMENTS

holding tones in the lower part of the harmony. A single example will suffice—a monologue for bass clarinet in A, unaccompanied, from Liszt's "Dante" Symphony: (Figure XXXI).

FIGURE XXXI.

XIII.—THE BASSOON.

The bassoon, the bass instrument of the oboe family, has a conical tube about nine feet long, which, to make it less unwieldy, is doubled upon itself in such a way that the instrument looks somewhat like a bundle of fagots—whence its Italian name, "Fagotto." Its double reed is connected with it by a bent brass tube for the convenience of the player. As in the oboe, the lower register is obtained by moderate breath-pressure, while increased pressure gives higher "partial" tones. The complete range is shown in Figure XXXII.

FIGURE XXXII.

RANGE AND QUALITIES OF THE BASSOON.

An excellent bass.   Best register for melodies.   Somewhat like 'cello tone, but thinner.

BASSOON

THE BASSOON

The bassoons are used in the orchestra for many purposes, chief of which are: (1) to provide or to reënforce the bass; (2) to "fill up" the harmony in the middle, for which their round yet unobtrusive tone well suits them; (3) to outline secondary melodic figures accompanying the chief melody; (4) to double a melody given out by some other instrument; (5) to give the melody alone.

There is an indescribable grotesqueness in the sound of the bassoon, especially when it is played *staccato,* that has earned for it the reputation of being "the clown of the orchestra." This is hardly fair to the versatility of the instrument; but it is certainly capable of being irresistibly ludicrous. Beethoven, of all composers the most humorous, has given the bassoon a prominent part in his most jovial symphony—the Eighth—examples from which are shown in Figure XXXIII. Mendelssohn,

FIGURE XXXIII.

(*a*) *Allegro vivace.*   BEETHOVEN: Eighth Symphony.
1st Bassoon.

etc.

(*b*) *Tempo di Menuetto.*   Ibid.

etc.

(*c*) *Allegro vivace.*   Ibid.

etc.

(1st Bassoon and Kettle-drums only.)

in his "Midsummer Night's Dream" music, has accompanied the entrance of Quince, Snug, Bottom, and the rest with a droll tune for two bassoons. M. Vincent d'Indy, in his "Wallenstein," suggests the sermon of a wordy priest by a fugue on the following theme, given out by bassoons:

FIGURE XXXIV.

VINCENT D'INDY: "Wallenstein."

There is also about the bassoon tone, however, a certain level drone, a bloodless indifference and lack of inflection, that can well suggest the inhuman and the terrifyingly supernatural. Such is the suggestion of a remarkable passage in Meyerbeer's "Robert le Diable"—the passage for two bassoons in the scene of the rising of the nuns:

FIGURE XXXV.

MEYERBEER: "Robert le Diable."

CONTRABASS CLARINET OR CONTRABASSOON

In our own day Tschaikowsky, for whom the murky, sinister coloring of chords in the extreme low register has a special fascination, has demonstrated new possibilities for this many-sided instrument in such passages as the following, from his "Pathetic Symphony":

FIGURE XXXVI.

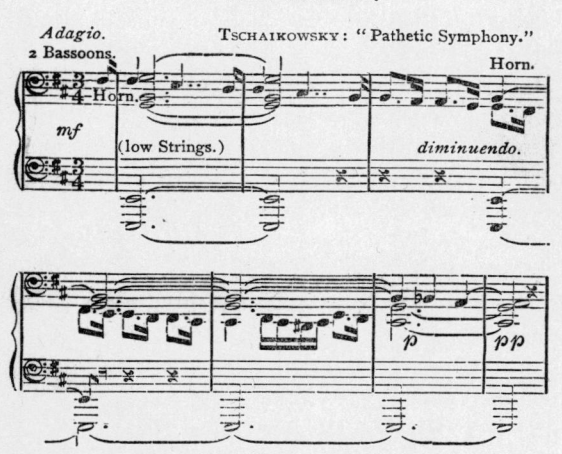

An instrument comparatively seldom employed in the orchestra is the contra-bassoon or contra-fagotto, related to the bassoon much as the double-bass is related to the violoncello. Its tube being twice as long, its pitch is one octave lower. Like the double-bass, it is written an octave higher than it sounds.

CHAPTER IV.

XIV.—THE BRASS INSTRUMENTS.

We come now to the third group of the orchestra, the brass instruments, of which the most important are horns, trumpets, trombones, and tuba. These all differ technically from the wood-wind instruments in one vital respect; they use many more of the partial tones produced by different wind-pressure, depending indeed chiefly on these, and not on changes in the length of the tube, for their alterations of pitch. They require, therefore, in the player, great delicacy and certainty in the management of the lips and breath—a complex muscular adjustment for which the technical name is "embouchure," from the French "bouche," mouth—which is the chief element in their technique. The false notes one frequently hears from the horns are the result of slight miscalculations of the needed embouchure, or of fatigue of the over-strained lip-muscles. That any one can play the horn at all is wonderful to the layman who has ever tried.

XV.—THE HORN.

Let us imagine a brass tube sixteen feet in length, curled over upon itself to save room and provided with a mouth-piece at one end and a flaring "bell" at the other. If the air-column

FRENCH HORN

THE HORN

contained in such a tube is now set in vibration by the lips of a player, it is capable of producing the whole series of tones shown in Figure XXXVII, which tone comes out depending

FIGURE XXXVII.

(*a*) SERIES OF PARTIAL TONES PRODUCIBLE IN A TUBE SIXTEEN FEET LONG.

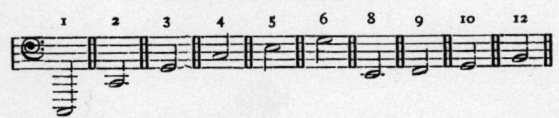

(*b*) AVAILABLE PARTIAL TONES OF A "NATURAL" HORN IN E FLAT.

on the force of the breath and the position of the lips. These tones are the partial tones, or overtones, of the low C, which is called the "fundamental" of the series. Such an instrument was the old-fashioned "horn in C" of the eighteenth and early nineteenth century, the type of the horns used by the great classic masters Haydn, Mozart, and Beethoven.

It will be noted that the seventh and the eleventh partial tones are omitted in the figure: this is because they are not in tune in the key (that is, not in its scale, being either too sharp or too flat in pitch), and are therefore useless. The partials above the twelfth are also omitted, because to produce them is an almost intolerable strain on the lips of the player. Furthermore, the fundamental or first partial cannot be produced with the mouthpiece used, and the second and third are rather difficult and seldom used. Hence the resources of the old "horn in C" were confined to the seven tones beginning with the fourth partial in Figure XXXVII, together with a few others which the player obtained by "stopping" the orifice of the horn with his hand, and which were therefore called "stopped" tones, and were of a slightly veiled quality.

In order to make the old-fashioned "natural" horn (so-called to distinguish it from the modern valve-horn, to be explained presently) available for other keys besides C, it was provided with small bent tubes of brass, called "crooks," which by being inserted in the instrument altered its length, and thus changed its pitch. If the music was in the key of E, the player used the proper crook to make his instrument into an "E horn"; if in B-flat, he used his B-flat crook, etc. But since it was highly necessary that a glance at the written note should tell him what embouchure was needed to produce it, no matter what its actual pitch might be, the horn part was always written in C, the necessary change of pitch being provided for by the indication at the beginning "Horn in E-flat," "Horn in F," etc.

This mode of notation is still used, so that the horn is a transposing instrument. The score-reader has to calculate what tone will actually be sounded by considering what crook is in use. Fortunately for him the horn in F is used almost universally nowadays, as being, all things considered, the easiest and best. Since a C sounds the F below it on this horn, the reader merely has to remember that the horn-part will sound a perfect fifth lower than it is written.

To return, however, to the old-fashioned horn. Even with its crooks, the "open tones" (that is, the partials of its natural series, unaltered by the hand) which it could sound were very few, and its limitations must often have been a sore trial to composers. Thus, for example, Beethoven, using in his Fifth Symphony two horns in E-flat, of which the open tones are shown in Figure XXXVII, *b,* introduces his second theme with a highly effective fanfare for horns alone, consisting of the twelfth, eighth, ninth, and sixth partial tones; but when, later, he wishes to repeat this fanfare in the key of C-major, he cannot get the necessary tones with his E-flat horns, and has to choose the lesser of two evils and give the passage to the bassoons, whose *timbre* is hardly appropriate to it. Nowadays, valve-horns being in use, this passage is played by them, much to its advantage.

As an example of what can nevertheless be done even with the old-fashioned horn may be cited a famous horn duet from Weber's "Freischütz" Overture (Figure XXXVIII). By

FIGURE XXXVIII.

Adagio. Horns in C.   WEBER: "Freischütz" Overture

Horns in F.   Horns in C.   1 Horn in F joins in.

using two pairs of horns, one in C and one in F, and cleverly dividing up the music between them, Weber manages to get a surprising variety of harmony and melody. Moreover, the passage is admirably conceived to display the round, full, and pure tone of the horn, which must ever be one of the most poetic of instruments.

The vastly increased resources of the modern horn are due to the introduction of the valves, undoubtedly one of the most epoch-making improvements in the entire history of the orchestra. The valves are three pistons, operated by the fingers of the player, which throw into the tube additional sections, thus lowering its pitch. They are so arranged that by their separate or combined use the pitch may be lowered anywhere from a semitone to three whole tones.

THE HORN

FIGURE XXXIX.

TECHNIQUE AND RANGE OF THE VALVE-HORN IN F.

Partial No. 4 5 6 8 9 10 12

"Open" tones.

With Piston 2.

With Piston 1.

With 3 (or 1 and 2).

With 2 and 3.

With 1 and 3.

With 1, 2 and 3.

Range, complete scale from [ ] to [ ]

with infrequently used lower partials (2 and 3).

A glance at Figure XXXIX will show what added possibilities this means. The first line of notes shows the "open" or natural tones of the horn in F which, as we have said, is the horn generally used to-day, from the fourth to the twelfth partial. The second line shows these tones lowered a semitone by means of the second piston. The third line shows them lowered a whole tone by means of the first piston.

The other lines show further lowerings by other pistons or combinations of pistons.

Altogether we thus get the complete range of tones shown in the same figure, to which may also be added the infrequently used second and third partial tones. Thanks to the valves and pistons, the horn is now as conspicuous for its wide availability as it has always been for nobility of tone.[1]

One last interesting fact about the complex technique of the horn is this: The embouchure for the low partials is so different from that for the high that few individual players can produce both. Hence the horns are divided into pairs, first and second, and third and fourth. The first and third players form the habit of producing the higher partials, the second and fourth become habituated to the lower; the composer bears this in mind in writing their parts.

The tone-quality of the horn is unforgettable to any one who has once heard it: sonorous and blaring in fortissimo, ominous, threatening in the "stopped tones," mysterious and poetic in pianissimo, its variety is almost unlimited, and can hardly be more than hinted at in the few examples which our space permits us. The horns, too, though more suitable for sustained

---

(1) Strauss, Mahler, and other modern composers sometimes use also the fifteenth and sixteenth partials, by which the range shown in Figure XXXIX is extended up to the F on the top line of the staff.

THE HORN

tones than for rapid figures, are used in a great variety of ways. They may merely sustain the harmonies, as they do with splendid sonority in the accompaniment to the melody of Tschaikowsky shown in Figure XII; they may intensify some one strand which needs to be salient; they may form an unaccompanied quartet or trio; and their full, clear tone is most effective in solos, either alone or doubling other instruments such as the 'cello, the clarinet, or the oboe.

FIGURE XL.

(a) Allegro vivace.   BEETHOVEN: Eroica Symphony.

(b) *Allegro con anima.*   Tschaikowsky: Fifth Symphony.

THE HORN

In Figure XL, the reader will find two interesting passages for horns used *en masse*: in Figure XLI are two not less striking horn solos. Figure XL, *a* is the beginning of the famous and inimitably beautiful trio from the scherzo of Beethoven's "Eroica" Symphony, of which Sir George Grove well said: "If horns ever talked like flesh and blood, they do it here." This entire trio should be examined in the score. The D-flat for the second horn near the end (it is written B-flat, as the horns are in E-flat) is certainly one of the most inspired things in all music.

Figure XL, *b*, in a very different style, is taken from the portion of Tschaikowsky's Fifth Symphony, the first movement, immediately preceding the return of the main theme. The gradual diminuendo of horns from loudest fortissimo to magical pianissimo, always most effective, is nowhere managed better than here, where its æsthetic effect is enhanced by the descent from D to C-sharp, and from C-sharp to C, and by the gradual subsidence of the rhythmic movement. The theme in E-minor, too, with its quaint suspensions, is eminently well-suited to the bassoon, and affords an additional example for that instrument.

In solo the horn is generally quiet and poetic. Our two examples, one from Tschaikowsky and one from Brahms, call for no special comment. It would not be difficult to cite many other examples from modern composers, with whom the horn is a favorite instrument.

FIGURE XLI.

(a) Andante cantabile. TSCHAIKOWSKY: Fifth Symphony.

(b) Poco allegretto. BRAHMS: Third Symphony.

XVI.—THE TRUMPET.

In many respects like the horn, the trumpet has a tube only half as long, and is therefore in pitch an octave higher. Like the horn, it is provided with crooks to change its general pitch, and with valves to give tones not pro-

TRUMPET

THE TRUMPET

vided for by its natural series of partials. This series of partials, on a trumpet in C, eight feet long, would be one octave higher than the series shown in Figure XXXVII,*a*. Like the horn, the trumpet cannot sound the fundamental tone (partial No. 1) and can sound only with great difficulty partials higher than the twelfth.

The usage of composers in the selection of the crooks differs: some use whenever possible trumpets in the key in which they are writing; others use almost invariably either the trumpet in A or that in B-flat, the transpositions of which are exactly like those of the A and B clarinets (see page 54). In our examples, however, as in those for the other transposing instruments, we shall write the tones just as they sound.

"The quality of tone of the trumpet," says Berlioz, "is noble and brilliant; it comports with warlike ideas, with cries of fury and of vengeance, as with songs of triumph; it lends itself to the expression of all energetic, lofty, and grand sentiments, and to the majority of tragic accents." The military associations of the instrument make themselves keenly felt in those fanfares for several trumpets together, of which Mendelssohn and Wagner have given such stirring specimens in their famous marches. Less frequently are they used for sustained melodies, but they are nevertheless highly effective in such use when the themes themselves are of triumphant or jubilant character. Dvořák gives to trumpets and horns, accompanied by great chords of the full orchestra on the accents, one of the themes of his "New World" Symphony (Figure XLII, *a*).

FIGURE XLII.

(*a*) *Allegro con fuoco.*   Dvořák: "New World" Symphony.
(2 Trumpets and 2 Horns.)

(1st Trumpet an octave higher.)

(*b*) *Allegro.*   Brahms: Academic Overture.

p dolce.   (Horn.)   (3rd Tr.)

pp (Kettledrum.)

(Bass trombone.)

The brilliantly sonorous quality of the trumpet tone in forte makes it easily stand out above all the other sounds of the full orchestra. Thus used, however, it is generally accompanied by ombones and tuba, and we shall therefore postpone our examples of this kind of passage until we have studied those instruments.

In its softer accents the trumpet is wonderfully clear, round, and pure, with a most imagination-stirring suggestion of distance and mystery. With high poetic fancy Schubert introduces, during one of the repetitions of the oboe theme of the slow movement of his C-major Symphony, a soft trumpet call which lends the music an indescribable charm. It is like a slender line of scarlet in a quiet colored painting. (Full score, Peters edition, page 43.) A not less lovely passage, for three trumpets, *piano,* from Brahms's "Academic" Overture is shown in Figure XLII,*b.*

XVII.—TROMBONES AND TUBA.

Though its name means in Italian "great trumpet," the trombone differs from the trumpet in two most important respects. First, the shape of the tube is such (see the illustration) that its lengthening can be managed by means of a section which slides in and out, instead of by means of valves and pistons (hence its name of "slide-trombone"[1]). Secondly, the tube is so much wider than in horn and trumpet that the rich first partial tone (fundamental) unavailable on those instruments, can be sounded. A slight compensating disadvantage is that the

---

(1) There is also a valve-trombone in common use in military bands, of which the tone is, however, far inferior to that of the orchestral instrument. "It will be an evil day for the orchestra," says Professor Prout, "if this instrument, easier to play, should ever supplant the noble slide trombone."

upper partials, above the eighth, are difficult and seldom used.

As the slide is capable of the most minute adjustments, the trombone need never be even slightly out of tune, as are certain tones of the horn and trumpet. Moreover, owing to its straight tube, free from those sharp corners introduced by valves, its air-column vibrates more evenly and regularly, giving it a sonority incomparably rich. For pure four-part harmony in simple chords there is no medium like the quartet of trombones.

FIGURE XLIII.

"Positions" and Range of the common Tenor Trombone.

TROMBONE

Range (exclusive of the rarely used "pedal notes"):

Range of the Bass Tuba:

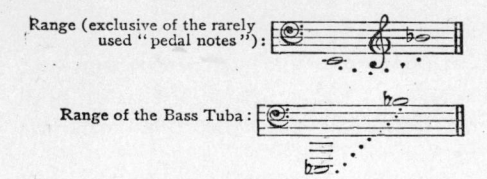

Trombones are made in various sizes, the most important of which is the tenor trombone in B-flat. This is of such proportions that when the slide is closed (which is called "first position") the tube gives out the first series of tones shown in Figure XLIII. Six other positions, obtained by gradually drawing out the slide, give the other series shown in the figure, each a semitone lower than the preceding, as in the series obtained on the horn by the use of valves (compare Figure XXXIX). The fundamental tones are easily obtainable only in the first four positions, and are seldom used.

There are also bass trombones having a range somewhat lower than the tenor, and there were formerly in use alto, and even soprano, trombones. The modern usage is however to write either for three tenor trombones, or for two tenors and a bass, to which are often added a part for the bass tuba, which will be described in a moment.

The trombones are not transposing instruments, but are written where they sound.

The bass tuba is an instrument of the saxhorn family (the other members of which are used only in military bands); its tone merges so well with that of trombones that it is often used

80 THE ORCHESTRAL INSTRUMENTS

with them to form a brass quartet. It is a valve-instrument of enormous proportions and very low pitch. The range of the most common tuba, sometimes called the Bombardon, is shown in Figure XLIII.

The three trombones and tuba, forming what we may call for convenience the trombone choir, constitute the most powerfully sonorous group of the entire orchestra, capable of dominating everything else. It must be confessed that this choir is often used vulgarly in modern scores, for the sake of mere noise; Prout cleverly remarks of it that "like charity, it covers a multitude of sins." Properly used, nevertheless, it is incomparably noble and moving. It "suggests to the imagination," says M. Gevaert, "the idea of a power strange to man, superior to man: a power sometimes benign, sometimes sinister, but always redoubtable."

FIGURE XLIV.

(a) *Allegro vivo.* TSCHAIKOWSKY: " Pathetic Symphony."
Min. score, p. 58.

4 Horns.

2 Trumpets.

3 Trombones and Tuba.

(N. B.—Strings and wood-wind fill up the rests.)

TUBA

(*b*) *Andante.*   Ibid, p. 233.

[Musical notation: 3 Trombones and Tuba, dynamics marked *p*, *pp*, *ppp*, *pppp*, *ppppp*]

We cite two examples from Tschaikowsky's greatest symphony (Figure XLIV), one *fortissimo* in a "tutti," the other *piano* and unaccompanied. In the first the trumpets play an octave higher than the upper trombones, while the four horns complete the harmony; this is an excellent illustration of the use of all the brass instruments in a "tutti," of which we postponed discussion above. The student will find it well worth while to play over the parts separately, and then imagine the combined effect.

In the great majority of "tuttis" the brass is grouped in close harmonies in somewhat this fashion, making a solid core of harmony in the sonorous middle register, to which high strings and wood-wind add brilliancy. This is the scheme in the climax of the same composer's Fifth Symphony, of which a page of the full score is reproduced in Figure XLVI.

Sometimes, again, the trombones or the trumpets are used alone, not to give full harmony but to blare forth some imposing theme. In the miniature score of the Pathetic Symphony the reader will find, at page 69, an extraordinarily impressive use of the trombones in this way, and at page 44 a similar use of the trumpets. Indeed this score exhibits model after model of what we may without undue paradox call the legitimately sensational use of the brass. One may also consult the scores of Wagner or of Richard Strauss, but not without finding some passages in which there is less music than noise.

KETTLEDRUMS

CHAPTER V.

XVIII.—PERCUSSION INSTRUMENTS.

By far the least important department of the orchestra is the group of percussion instruments, many fine works not employing them at all. They are divided, as we saw in Section II, into two classes, according as the vibration is started by stretched membranes or by metallic bodies. The most important members of the first class are the kettledrums or "timpani" and the bass-drum; the most important of the second class are the cymbals.

The kettledrums, hemispheres of copper over which are stretched parchment "heads" capable of adjustment by screws, have the great advantage over other drums that they can give forth definite tones instead of mere noises. Two kettledrums, general tuned to the tonic and dominant, are found in the classic orchestra; three or four, often tuned for special effects, and even retuned in the course of a movement, are used by modern composers.

While the most constant function of the kettledrums is to add their throb to the excitement of "tuttis," they are capable of delightful effects in piano and pianissimo, either alone or as a bass for light combinations. Beethoven first discerned all their possibilities in this direction, and his symphonies abound in interesting kettledrum passages.

84 THE ORCHESTRAL INSTRUMENTS

Since Beethoven the quasi-solo use of the kettledrums is not infrequent. Let it suffice, however, to quote one striking example—the announcement in Wagner's "Walküre" of the Hunding motive by one kettledrum, almost unaccompanied (Figure XLV).

FIGURE XLV.

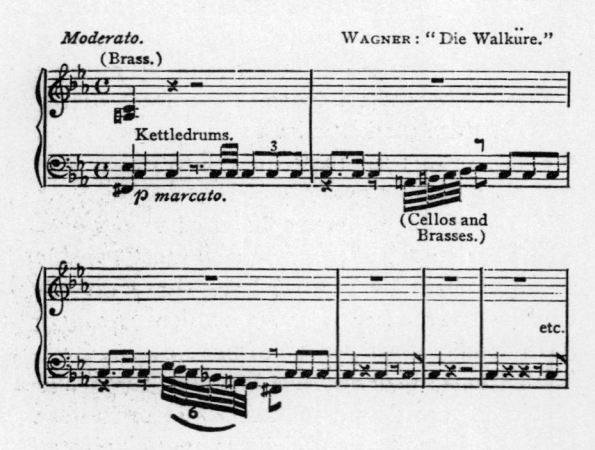

The bass drum, which has been made so familiar by the Salvation Army as to need no description, gives out no definite tone and is used merely for rhythmical accentuation. When played forte, especially if combined, as it often is, with the cymbals, it can very easily be abused, but in piano and pianissimo it is capable of fine effects. It is most subtly used, for example, at the beginning of Brahms's "Academic Overture."

PERCUSSION INSTRUMENTS

The cymbals are two disks of metal which when struck together emit a noisy but most exciting clangor. They are usually employed with the bass-drum, though Wagner in the "Tannhäuser" Overture, uses them alone for the Venusberg music. They may also be played *piano,* and a very happy effect is sometimes obtained by striking one suspended cymbal with a drum-stick.

The triangle is a small bar of steel, bent as its name suggests, and struck by a steel rod. It emits a delicate, ethereal tinkle, especially delightful in soft dance music.

The glockenspiel is a series of metal bars, emitting definite tones when struck by hammers in the fashion made familiar by the xylophone dear to children.

The gong, or tamtam, of Chinese origin, a large metal disk played with a bass-drum stick, is the most sinister of all the percussion instruments, and is used only in highly dramatic moments.

CHAPTER VI.

XIX.—ORCHESTRAL COMBINATIONS.

The possible combinations of orchestral instruments are practically infinite. Even to hint at their extraordinary variety would be impossible within the limits of the present discussion; nevertheless, so important a matter as orchestral combinations must be at least touched upon here, however inadequately.

Merely to get a glimpse of the bewildering possibilities, let us suppose we wish to orchestrate a single melody, without accompaniment. Without going beyond the wood-wind instruments we can find the following excellent combinations for it: (1) flutes and oboes, in octaves or in unison; (2) flutes and clarinets, in octaves or in unison; (3) oboes and clarinets (best in unison); (4) flutes and bassoons, two octaves apart (a favorite medium with Mozart); (5) oboes and bassoons in octaves (infrequent but possible); (6) clarinets and bassoons, in octaves, common and excellent; (7), flutes, clarinets, and bassoons, playing in three octaves simultaneously. This without going beyond the wood-wind group, and with a single melody. If we add the horns, trumpets, trombones, and strings, the resources are amazing.

It may be said in passing that single melodies in orchestral music are more often given in

SNARE DRUM

octaves than in unison, in order better to fill the large canvas, so to speak. Fine effects are, however, possible in unison: an extreme case is the opening theme of Bizet's L'Arlesienne Suite, played by English horn, clarinets, alto saxophone, bassoons, horns, first and second violins, violas, and violoncellos, not in octaves but *in unison*. The tone thus produced is of remarkable sonority—what the French call a "well-nourished" tone.

Passing over the possible combinations of two and three melodies or "parts" ("voices") sounding at once, making what is called two and three-part harmony, we come to the more usual combination of four parts, of which the prototype is the vocal quartet of soprano, alto, tenor, and bass. Without going beyond the wood-wind and horns, we can get the following quartets for such four-part harmony: (1) flutes and clarinets; (2) clarinets and bassoons—(these are the commonest four-part combinations); (3) oboes and clarinets, which do not mix quite so well, but can be most effective, especially if the two pairs of instruments "straddle," that is if the upper clarinet is written above the lower oboe; (4) oboes and horns; (5) clarinets and horns; (6) bassoons and horns. The strings and the brass are also capable of many varying four-part combinations, and of course there are endless cross-combinations between the various groups.

"Tutti" passages are as a general rule built up on four-part harmony, many instruments merely "doubling" others, either in unison or at a distance of one or more octaves. In the music of Haydn and Mozart we frequently find chords in which the strings, playing four-part harmony, are doubled by the wood-wind, the horns and trumpets usually being given the most important tone of the chord, on account of their prominence. In another kind of "tutti" we may find the strings bunched low down, the wood-wind playing the same tones in higher octaves: in such cases the wood-wind instruments are frequently not heard individually but simply add brightness to the quality of the strings, merging with them as overtones merge with their fundamentals.

In the "tuttis" of modern works the arrangement is often a very different one, for two reasons. In the first place, the great increase in the number of brass instruments in modern orchestras has given to this department such powerful sonority that no single pair of wind instruments, nor even a single group of strings such as the second violins or violas, can balance it. Consequently a division of each group in four parts, such as we find in older scores, would be ineffective. In the second place, modern composers have so keen a sense of tone-color that they prefer a distinct color for each part or voice to the mingling of colors obtained by the older method. They accordingly give one part entirely to the strings, playing in several octaves the same notes, another part to the wood-wind, doubled in the same way, and a third to the brass.

CYMBALS

ORCHESTRAL COMBINATIONS

An example will make this clear. Figure XLVI shows the full score of one of the climaxes in the first movement of Tschaikowsky's Fifth Symphony. In the second measure the harmony is what is technically called the six-four chord of E-major, viz. B, E, G-sharp, B. Now notice the way the instruments are divided. The E and the G-sharp are entrusted entirely to the powerful brasses, four horns (their notes written a fifth higher than they sound) and two trombones. In order to make themselves heard against this formidable array of brass, all the strings are concentrated on the tone B, giving it four different octaves; they are moreover further re-enforced by flutes and piccolo, clarinets, and first bassoon. The low B is taken by doublebasses, drums, second bassoon, third trombone, and tuba. The oboes and trumpets are withheld in order to enter on another "part" at the fourth measure.

Had Tschaikowsky been using only two instead of four horns, and no trombones and tuba, he would not have found it necessary to muster so many instruments on the high B. He might then have doubled his horns with his clarinets and bassoons, possibly also with his violas and violoncellos. This matter of balance of tone, as it is called, is one of the most important and interesting in orchestration; mastery of it comes to a composer only as the result of long experience, and even the masters sometimes miscalculate, as does Schubert for example, near the end of the first movement of

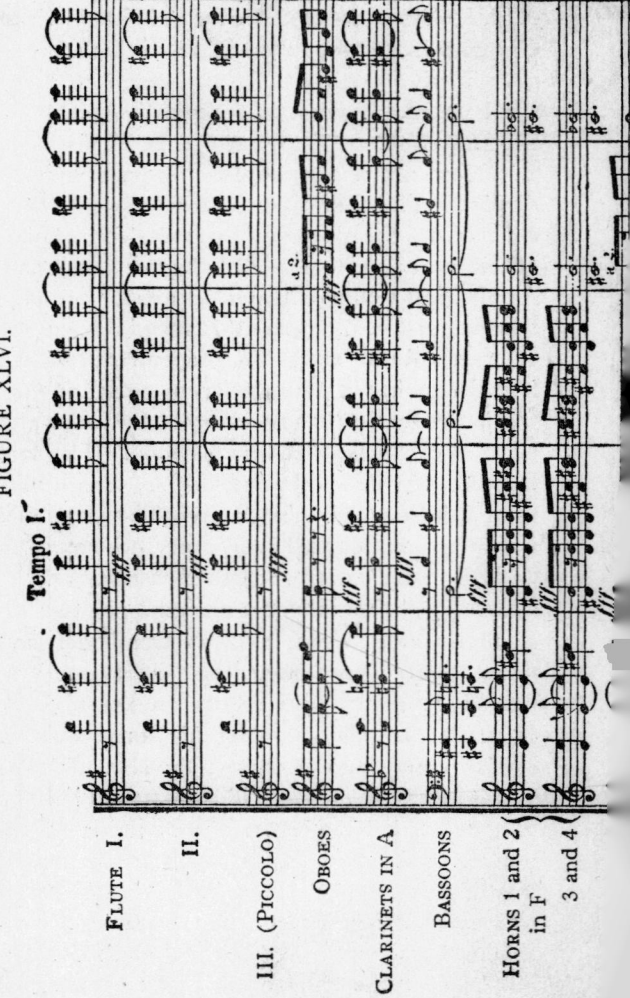

FIGURE XLVI.

ORCHESTRAL COMBINATIONS 91

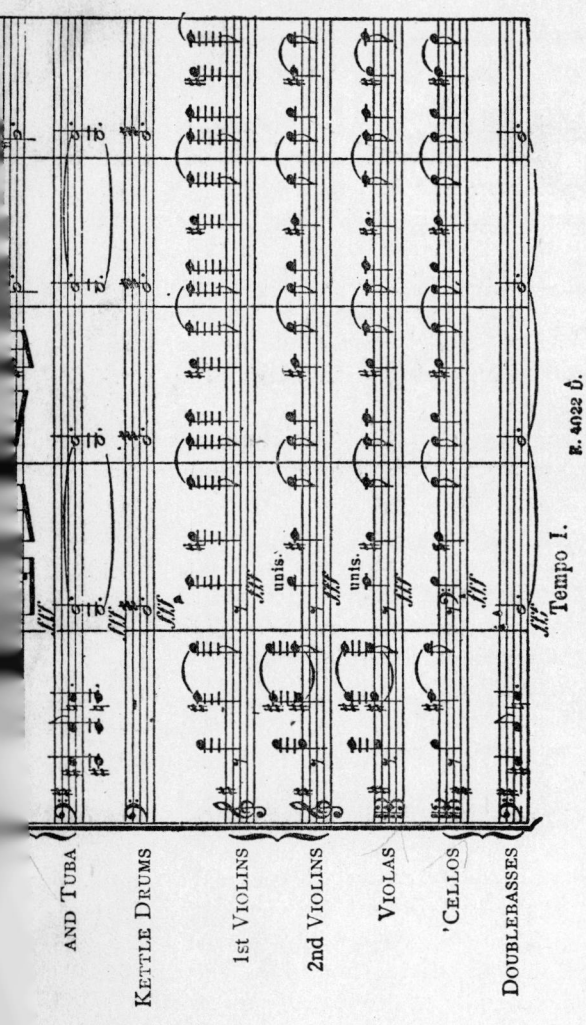

FROM THE 5TH SYMPHONY. TSCHAIKOWSKY.

his C-major Symphony, where he smothers his theme, assigned to wood-wind and horns, under a too heavy mass of strings, trombones, and drums.

Even in passages where the whole orchestra is not employed, modern composers often assign each harmonic part to a special group of instruments instead of dividing the parts up among the various instruments of the several groups after the fashion of the classical writers. This, as we suggested above, is largely due to their love of strongly marked tone-color, since this method of scoring achieves wondrous clarity and contrast.

Those who own the miniature score of Tschaikowsky's Fifth Symphony will find a striking instance at page 21. Here the texture of the music consists of a chief melody (the second theme of the movement), a subsidiary melodic figure, a "filling-up" part, and the bass. These four parts might have been divided up among the strings, and suitably re-enforced by wood-wind doublings, but such a treatment would have been dull and lifeless in comparison with the one Tschaikowsky adopts. By giving the main melody to violins alone, in two octaves, and the subsidiary figures to flutes, oboes, clarinets, and bassoons, in three octaves, he gets a complete contrast between the tone-colors of the two designs, by virtue of which each stands out in a splendid saliency. Both in its daring and in its success this method of scoring reminds one of the impressionistic

TRIANGLE

painter's use of unmixed pigments, set side by side on the canvas.

The ineffectiveness of Schumann's orchestration, so much discussed by critics, is largely due to loss of purity of colors through injudicious mixing (doubling). His method is in this respect at the opposite pole from that of Tschaikowsky. He seems afraid to entrust a melody to any one instrument, and forgets that by doubling it with an instrument of different family he loses as much in purity of color as he gains in volume of sound. Through this persistent mixture of colors the relief of contrast is lost, and the clearness of the design is apt to suffer as much as the charm of the material.

One other principle of orchestration deserves a word here. Just as the lines or melodies, on the clearness and grace of which the beauty of the music chiefly depends, may be dangerously obscured by too great similarity of tone-color, they may also obscure one another by getting too near together. The ear's power to distinguish tones in a single region of pitch is limited. For this reason it would be most unwise to place a melody and its accompaniment in the same register. On the other hand, it would be monotonous to place it always above its accompaniment. In the best scores, then, we find the melody sometimes above, sometimes below, but always clearly separated from its accompaniment, either in register or by contrast of tone-color.

The works of Dvořák, who is much addicted to accompaniments above the melody, may be consulted by those anxious to study further this phase of orchestration.

GLOCKENSPIEL

CHAPTER VII.

XX.—SCORES AND SCORE-READING.

Music-lovers who have had little practice in reading music are apt to fancy themselves quite unable to get anything from the complicated pages of a full score. With its many staves, its various clefs, and its mysterious appearance of being in several keys at the same time, it is indeed at first bewildering; nevertheless with a little study the veriest tyro can gather from it much information, much stimulus to closer attention and keener delight. Now that most of the classical symphonies and the best modern works can be obtained in miniature scores that fit in the pocket and cost little, there is no excuse for those who do not learn something about this fascinating department of music.

Let us suppose a person who knows nothing whatever about music (to take an extreme case), but likes it and wants to learn what he can of the orchestra. First of all, he must spend fifteen minutes over some simple account of time in music, the note-values, counting, the accent, the difference between double and triple time, etc. Next, he knows that tones are represented by the notes on the staff, that when these get higher the tones "go up," when they get lower the tones "come down," when they are wide apart there is a jump in the melody, etc., etc. Now let him take up the score of a symphony he is to hear performed.

He will notice that the various groups of instruments are assigned different parts of the page. The five lines at the bottom are the strings, the nucleus of the orchestra, and the most important staff in the entire score is that fifth one from the bottom—that of the first violins. The wood-wind is at the top of the page, generally in this order: flutes, oboes, clarinets, bassoons; the bass clef of the bassoon part is a means of locating at a glance the line separating wood from brass. In the middle of the page comes the brass; one or two staves for horns, one for trumpets, and two for trombones and tuba. Between brass and strings are noted the percussion instruments, usually merely kettledrums.

The next step is to get some idea of what is going on. For this purpose the great clue for our tyro is the time. As the orchestra plays, let him count with it, being sure that "one" always comes on the accent. Then if he simply remembers the note-values, and bears in mind that whatever instrument has the melody at any given moment will show a more solid, continuous line of notes than the others, he will be able to follow on after a fashion. Of course he will get no very definite ideas at first: if he manages to keep up at all he will do well; even better if he manages to tell when the melody is in the hands of a stringed instrument, when of a wood or brass. But with repeated trials he will be gratified to find that he learns more each time, constantly discovering new beauties.

TAMTAM

SCORES AND SCORE-READING

Eventually the neophyte may find himself sufficiently interested to "learn his notes" and to acquire some degree of proficiency in hearing with the eye, as it has been called; that is, in the ability to form a mental image of melodies and chords noted on paper. One possessed of such powers can of course get much more from a score than he who follows only rhythms and up-and-down motion of melodies. At the same time he will find his difficulties increased by the varying clefs and by the transpositions, to which the other need pay no attention. For the sake of this more careful reader the various disconcerting tricks of the instruments, in the order in which they occur in the score, may now be briefly recapitulated.

Flutes. Sound as written. Piccolo or small flute sounds an octave higher. (N. B. in the Tschaikowsky score shown in Figure XLVI the first two staves are for the two flutes, the third for the piccolo.) The two flutes are usually written on one staff. The abbreviation "*a 2*" indicates that both play the notes written; the Roman numerals I or II indicate that either the first or the second flute plays.

Oboes. Sound as written.

Clarinets. B-flat clarinet sounds a major second lower than written: A clarinet a minor third lower. In Figure XLVI, the symphony being in E-minor, Tschaikowsky uses A clarinets playing in G-minor; hence the signature of two flats in the clarinet part.

Bassoons. Sound as written. The F-clef

is used for the lower registers, for the higher the tenor clef which makes the fourth line of the staff middle C.

Horns. If F-horns are used the parts will be written a fifth higher than they sound. No signature, however, is used in the horn part, all the accidentals being written in as they occur. If other than F-horns are used one can easily calculate the transposition by bearing in mind that the note written C will sound the tone for which the horn is named, and that this note will in every case be *below* that written. There are, however, two different horns in B-flat: the horn in B-flat *alto* sounds a major second lower than written; that in B-flat *basso* sounds a major ninth lower.

Trumpets. If A or B-flat crooks are used the transposition is exactly as in the similar clarinets (see page 97). In all the other trumpets in common use the transposition can be calculated on the principle just suggested for the horn, viz., by bearing in mind that the note written C will sound the tone for which the trumpet is named. These tones, however, in the case of the trumpet, are *above* instead of below the note written. No signature is used for the trumpet part.

Trombones. The first and second trombones are usually written with the tenor clef, bringing middle C on the fourth line. The third trombone and tuba are written on a second staff with the ordinary F-clef.

Kettledrums. Written where they sound.

TAMBOURINE

CASTANETS

SCORES AND SCORE-READING

Violins. Written where they sound.

Viola. The alto clef is used, bringing middle C on the third line.

Violoncello. When the 'cello goes very high the tenor clef is sometimes used, or even the G-clef.

Double-bass. Sounds an octave lower than written.

APPENDIX.

Orchestral Chart, Showing the Ranges and Qualities of the Orchestral Instruments in Relation to the Pianoforte Keyboard.

(See Frontispiece.)

The object of this chart is to present in compact form, for easy reference, the main facts as to the ranges, and qualities in various registers, of the commonly used orchestral instruments. As several different clefs are used in writing for these instruments, and as many of them are "transposing instruments" (*i. e.,* sounding higher or lower than written), it is not at all an easy matter to gain from books on orchestration a clear idea of their relations, such as is afforded here by representing the actual sounds of all instruments as they compare with those of the piano.

The instruments are here arranged in the order in which they are found in orchestral scores: at the top of the chart are the wood-wind instruments, extending down to the first heavy double line; then come the brass instruments, extending to the next double line; and finally the strings, extending from there to the keyboard. After finding the name of any

APPENDIX

instrument you wish to investigate, note the lines which indicate the limits of its range; follow these down to the keyboard by means of the guiding lines; thus you find the entire range. The transverse lines divide this range up into registers, each of which is characterized by a descriptive phrase.

In some instruments the limits of the range, depending somewhat on the skill of the player, are variable. In such cases it must be understood that the limits shown on the chart may sometimes be exceeded; the author's plan has been to give the conservative range in each case, such as may be expected from average players in average orchestras.

A few explanatory notes on each instrument follow:

PICCOLO. The lowest octave of the range is weak, the tones being much better on the flute. The best register is the second octave. Above that the tone is piercing, and can be produced only in fortissimo.

The piccolo sounds an octave higher than written.

FLUTE. The best register for quiet solo passages is the middle. The upper register is brilliant. The lower tones are little used save for special dramatic effects.

OBOE. The middle register is capable of great variety of expression. The lower cannot be had in piano or pianissimo. The oboe is less agile than the flute and clarinet. Its tone is peculiarly penetrating, so that the tones given to it in a chord for wood-wind instruments stand out with special prominence.

102 THE ORCHESTRAL INSTRUMENTS

ENGLISH HORN. Really not a horn at all, but an alto oboe. Melancholy and sombre in its lower register: the upper little used.

CLARINET. Two clarinets are in common use, the clarinet in B-flat, and the clarinet in A. The first sounds a major second lower than written, the second a minor third lower.

The lower register, called the "chalumeau" after an obsolete wind instrument, is peculiarly full and mellow. Then comes a break in which the tone is dull and the fingering difficult. Above this is more than an octave of clear, fine tones; as the upper limit of the range is approached these gradually become shrill.

BASS-CLARINET. Made in B-flat and in A, like the ordinary instrument, but sounding an octave lower. The lower two octaves are of excellent, full tone; the upper register is seldom used, being better on the ordinary clarinet.

The bass-clarinet in B-flat sounds a major ninth lower than written.

BASSOON. The bass of the wood-wind instruments. Lower register sonorous; upper good for melodies, though somewhat veiled and mysterious; highest notes thin.

DOUBLE-BASSOON. Used only for bass, or for melodic phrases in low register.

This instrument, sometimes called contrafagotto, sounds an octave lower than written.

HORN IN F. The horn in commonest use is that in F, sounding a fifth lower than written. As the "embouchure" (tension of the lips and pressure of breath) varies for different parts of the range, the horns are arranged in pairs, the first horn playing higher than the second, third higher than the fourth, etc. (See the chart.)

For the lowest notes, the F-clef is sometimes used, but the notes are then, rather illogically, written an octave lower, so that instead of being a fifth higher than the sounds produced, they are a fourth lower.

APPENDIX

Other horns sometimes used, and their transpositions, are as follows:

HORN IN B-Flat Alto.   Sounds a major second lower than written.
"   " **A**   Sounds a minor third lower.
"   " **A-Flat**   Sounds a major third lower.
"   " **G**   Sounds a perfect fourth lower.
"   " **E**   Sounds a minor sixth lower.
"   " **E-Flat**   Sounds a major sixth lower.
"   " **D**   Sounds a minor seventh lower.
"   " **C**   Sounds an octave lower.
"   " **B-Flat Basso**   Sounds a major ninth lower.

TRUMPET IN B-FLAT. The B-flat trumpet is the most popular with players. Like the horns, the trumpets are arranged in pairs, the first of each pair taking the higher tones and the second the lower. The extreme upper notes shown on the chart are difficult, and seldom used. A few lower tones than the lowest shown are possible, but extremely rare, not being of good quality.

The trumpet in B-flat sounds a major second lower than written.

Other trumpets, and their transpositions, are as follows:

TRUMPET IN F.   Sounds a fourth higher than written.
"   " **E**   Sounds a major third higher.
"   " **E-Flat**   Sounds a minor third higher.
"   " **D**   Sounds a major second higher.
"   " **C**   Sounds as written.
"   " **A**   Sounds a minor third lower.

The higher the pitch of the instrument, the more difficult are the upper tones.

The trumpet has unfortunately been supplanted in many of our orchestras by the cornet, an instrument of inferior tone, but easier to play. The cornet in B-flat has practically the same range as that shown for the trumpet. It is written a major second higher than it sounds. The A cornet, a half tone lower than the B-flat, is of course written a minor third higher than it sounds. These two are the only cornets in ordinary use.

TENOR TROMBONE. The most sonorous register is that lying just above and below middle C, as shown on the chart. Below the regular range, after a slight gap, there are a few so-called "pedal notes."

The trombone parts are written as sounded, but for the higher notes the tenor clef is used, which places middle C on the fourth line of the staff.

The bass trombone has the same range a minor third lower.

TUBA. The tuba in most common use, sometimes called the Bombardon, has the range shown in the chart, is used as the bass of the trombone choir, and is written as it sounds, in the F-clef. There is also a "tuba in B-flat," or Euphonium, pitched a fifth higher, and a Contrabass tuba, pitched a fourth lower. The "Serpent" and the "Ophicleide" are obsolete instruments which used to take the place now occupied by the tuba.

VIOLIN. The violins in the orchestra are divided into two groups, first violins and second violins. Both are written as they sound, with the common G-clef.

VIOLA. The viola is a non-transposing instrument, but its lower notes are written with the alto clef, which places middle C on the third line of the staff.

VIOLONCELLO. Violoncello parts are written with the F-clef, the tenor clef (see trombone), and the G-clef. In many scores the notes written with the G-clef are notated an octave higher than they sound.

DOUBLE-BASS. The double-bass part is written an octave higher than it sounds.

785
M39 Mason
Ao   Orchestral instrumen

16654 43002
17021 1253
23 Jan '34   13 Dec '43
27405   1233
8 Feb   27 Dec
26896 5026
         6 Jan '45
16 Nov   B2490
30791   10 Jul '45
39990   DEC 5 1980
30 Nov '37   DEC 03 '82
         APR 05 1985
33503
14 Feb '38
57869   APR 03 1986
         JAN 11 1993
         DEC 27 1994

NOV 02 1999
JUN 30 2000

munteni

WITHDRAWN